First published in the UK by Sweet Cherry Publishing Limited, 2024
Unit 36, Vulcan House, Vulcan Road,
Leicester, LE5 3EF, United Kingdom

Nauschgasse 4/3/2 POB 1017
Vienna, WI 1220, Austria

2 4 6 8 10 9 7 5 3 1

ISBN: 978-1-80263-150-0

Football Rising Stars: Jordyn Huitema

Text by Harry Meredith
Illustrations by Sophie Jones

www.sweetcherrypublishing.com

Printed and bound in India

FOOTBALL RISING STARS

JORDYN HUITEMA

THE UNOFFICIAL STORY

Written by

HARRY MEREDITH

Sweet Cherry

CONTENTS

1

THE DECIDING GOAL

On the 4th of June 2021, Paris Saint-Germain were one match away from winning the top division of French football. A strong and talented side, PSG (nicknamed Les Parisiens) were

frequently competing at the top of the table. Despite this, the side had never won it before. They had never felt the glory and success of being crowned as league champions. But going into the final matchday of the 2020/2021 season, they had a chance. The team held their fate in their own hands, and they held a one point advantage over their nearest rivals: Olympique Lyon – a side that had won the league an astonishing

 fourteen years on the bounce. They had a chance of making it

fifteen, but it was not up to them. If PSG won their final game, they would secure the crown for themselves.

Instead of playing for the title in a stadium filled with thousands of cheering fans, the match had to take place in a near empty stadium. With the tie happening after COVID-19, restrictions were still in place and fans were not yet able to attend crowded events. The fans would be watching or listening from home, stuck on the edges of their seats with their fingers crossed, hoping that their team could get the job done and claim the Division 1 title.

PSG's opponents for the match were Dijon, a side that did not have anything to play for on the day other than pride. All Dijon could do was earn more points for themselves on the leaderboard and potentially play a key role in deciding where the title went. But no matter their position, the team were not going to roll over and allow PSG to easily claim the title. If PSG wanted it, they would have to pass a tough test against Dijon first.

In order to win, PSG would need their talented squad to play to the best of their ability. PSG had a host of stars in their starting lineup, such as Grace Geyoro, Kadidiatou Diani, Irene Paredes, Sara Däbritz and Ashley Lawrence. Not to mention a bench that was packed with players who could make an impact too. One of those stars was a young forward called Jordyn Huitema, a twenty-year-old from Canada who had earned her

reputation as one of the league's most promising young talents. The forward had made her contributions to the side, scoring and assisting over the team's long campaign. As the referee blew her whistle, Jordyn watched on. She hoped that her team could win the match and made sure that she would be ready if they needed her today.

PSG started brightly. Their early attacks were too much for Dijon to handle, and in the 8th minute Les Parisiens had earned themselves a penalty. Däbritz stepped up to take the spot kick and fired the ball into the right-hand corner. The goalkeeper guessed the right way but was unable to get her hands to the well-placed shot. Jordyn celebrated with her teammates on the bench. Däbritz ran over to the substitutes and high-fived them before running back onto the pitch. Jordyn's team were 1-0 up, but it was far too early to get carried away. Even though it had been an incredible start, there was still a lot of work for PSG to do.

Dijon tried their best to equalise, but they struggled to get past a strong PSG defence. Time started to tick away in the second half, and in the 60th minute PSG had a chance. The ball was crossed into the box from a corner and the club's captain, Paredes, rose highest. She met the ball with her forehead and fired it into the back of the net, giving the team a more comfortable 2-0 lead.

In the 68th minute, the PSG manager decided that it was time to put some fresh legs on the pitch. Nadia Nadim was taken out of the game and Jordyn was substituted on. She was given the task of keeping the opposition defenders busy and giving her all to help get the match over the

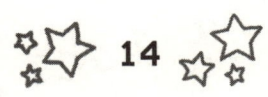

line. Jordyn did exactly that, as she was a constant nuisance for the Dijon defence. She made them sit back and worry about her attacking threat, rather than creating one of their own. With time in the match running out, it was clear which way the game was going. However, for every second that ticked by, Jordyn was going to give her all – no matter whether the game was wrapped up or not. And in the 90th minute, Jordyn's pressure paid off. Sandy Baltimore teased the tired Dijon defenders, before crossing the ball into the penalty area.

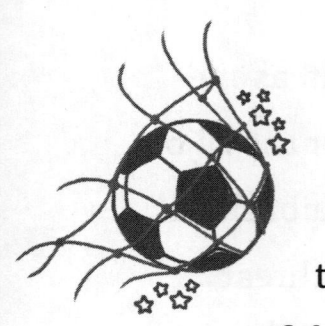

The accurate cross was met with a powerful header from Jordyn, and the ball flew into the back of the net. The score was 3-0, and PSG were only moments away from winning the team's first ever Division 1 title and making history.

In the other match of the day, Olympique Lyon had put up a strong fight in an attempt to retain their crown. But their 8-0 victory against Fleury 91 was not enough, because in Paris the final whistle had blown and PSG had won the match. Jordyn and her teammates celebrated, recognising that the hard work and effort they had all put in throughout the year had turned into success. Their goals, assists and clean sheets had resulted in medals and a trophy.

Jordyn might not have played in every match or scored the most goals for her team, but she was a player who could make a difference – as her goal had proved. She was a player who deserved to be enjoying victories and winning titles. All this at such a young age, and with so much of her career still ahead of her. If this was what Jordyn could achieve at the start of her career, there was no telling just how many medals, trophies and goals she could achieve in the future. She was one of the world's most exciting attacking prospects, and she had no plans to slow down any time soon.

2
CHILLIWACK
FC

Jordyn Huitema was raised in a
household filled with laughter, sport
and play. She was born to two athletic
parents on the 8th of May 2001 in
Chilliwack, British Columbia, which
is an area of Canada known for its
natural beauty and recreational spots.

Jordyn's parents, Roger and Julie, got involved with sporting activities whenever they could. Julie was an  excellent swimmer, while Roger dabbled in multiple sports. The Huitemas were a family who enjoyed getting the chance to play and compete against one another, taking advantage of the beautiful surroundings near their home to get active.

Jordyn grew up with two brothers, one older and one younger, who loved to play sports. Trent and Brody often spent their time playing in

the backyard, and Jordyn couldn't help but get swept up in the fun and excitement. With her brothers, Jordyn would get stuck into activities and keep herself busy and entertained for hours on end. But although Jordyn and her family played many different sports, there was one in particular that she started to like just a little bit more. Jordyn was hooked on football.

When Jordyn was just four years old, it became apparent to her parents that their daughter loved to play football. To help her take that passion further, they arranged for her to join a local football team. Jordyn became a member of Chilliwack FC and spent as much time as she possibly could on the football pitch, honing her skills and having a great time with new friends and coaches.

However, unlike others, Jordyn never entered the world of football with hopes and expectations for the future. She didn't immediately dream of making it a career or pursuing it any further. To Jordyn, football was just an incredibly fun sport

to play with friends. And
it was with this attitude
that Jordyn continued to play
football, growing and learning while
having a hobby that kept her happy
and active. Jordyn played with her
friends at Chilliwack FC until the age
of eleven.

Even though Jordyn only saw
football as a hobby, it was undeniable
to anyone who watched her that she
had a knack for it. As she rose through
the Chilliwack age groups, it was all
becoming far too easy for Jordyn. So,
to give herself a new challenge, she

asked to join the boys' team because there weren't as many competitive opportunities in the girls' team. After joining, she received a few funny looks from players and parents. Some of the boys found it odd that a girl was playing on their team, but these apprehensions and judgements were soon forgotten when they realised just how good Jordyn was. She swiftly transformed from just some girl who had joined the team to one of their best players, showing any doubters that football was a sport that could be played by anyone.

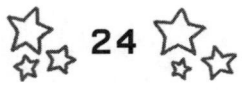

It was clear that Jordyn was a talented player. She was often the most eye-catching of everyone on the pitch and made an impact in games and training sessions. Her love for the game seeped into her every action on the field and was obvious to all who witnessed it. She would run further, try harder and do it all with a beaming smile on her face. Jordyn might not have realised it, but day by day she was developing her abilities to a point where her talent simply couldn't be ignored.

3
BRONZE FOR CANADA

Despite her talent, Jordyn still treated football as a pastime rather than anything serious. She participated in multiple sports outside of school, meaning that her spare time was often filled with exercise and activities.

Apart from football, the main sport that she spent her time playing was ice hockey. Ice hockey was an incredibly popular sport in Canada, and Jordyn enjoyed getting the opportunity to put on her skates and head to the ice rink. She loved flying across the ice at super-fast speeds, fighting to control the hockey puck and score.

Competing in multiple sports had many positives. The skills Jordyn learnt were transferable from one sport to the next, the regular exercise meant that

 her fitness levels were constantly improving, and the toughness of competitive matches in both football and ice hockey instilled a winning mentality. Jordyn loved every moment she spent on football pitches and ice rinks. But, as always with sport, the time soon came for her to choose between them. If an individual wants to become an expert in one sport, they have to dedicate every spare moment to it. This is the only way to put themselves in the best position to make it in a competitive

world where millions often have the same ambition: to be a professional in the sport that they love so much.

Jordyn was finding it difficult to choose, but during the summer of 2012 an event took place that inspired her – an event that she was mesmerised by.

That year, the Summer Olympic Games were being held in London, England. The Olympics were a festival and celebration of all kinds of sport, and it was where the world's best came together to compete against one

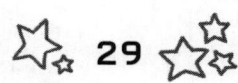

another in search of sporting glory – to chase a bronze, silver or elusive gold medal for their country. One of the team sports that was included in the Olympics was football. Countries from across the globe would be competing for the right to be known as Olympic champions. Canada had been placed in Group F, where they'd be competing against Japan, South Africa and Sweden. Despite the eight-hour time difference between Canada and England, Jordyn tried

her best to watch every minute of the
Canadian women's team competing
for Olympic glory.

Unfortunately, Canada's opening
match of the tournament didn't go
well. They lost a closely contested
game against Japan, which ended
in a 2-1 defeat. However, this
disappointment was the push they
needed to make it further in the
competition. The second match, a
game against South Africa, was
an entirely different
story. Canada ran
rings around their

opponents with a 3-0 victory, putting their campaign back on track. This was followed by a 2-2 draw against Sweden in the final group match, a result that was just enough to help the team progress to the knock-out rounds. Canada had finished third in their group, not in the group winners or runners up spot – the two

 positions ordinarily needed to progress from a tournament group. But in this competition, the two best teams that finished in third place also qualified for the knock-out rounds.

Canada's tournament was not over yet, and Jordyn felt hopeful that her team were still in with a chance of winning a medal.

Canada's next stop in the tournament was the quarter-finals, and it would be a difficult match. Canada were going to play against Great Britain, the hosts of the Olympics and a side that would be supported ferociously by thousands of home fans. Despite this home advantage, Canada were able to cause an upset and claim the victory, winning the match 0-2 and eliminating the hosts. The team had overcome an enormous hurdle, but what was to come next was even bigger. In the semi-finals, Canada had been drawn against the USA. These two countries were fierce sporting rivals, sharing both a border and cultural similarities with one another. Jordyn couldn't keep her eyes off the TV as the teams walked out of the tunnel and onto the pitch for this momentous occasion.

The match lived up to the hype, and the game finished with an

astonishing 4-3 scoreline. Canada's
leading striker, Christine Sinclair,
one of Jordyn's sporting idols, scored
a hat-trick in the match. But it wasn't
enough. Regular time ended with
the scoreline at 3-3, and the match
had to be decided in extra time.
Unfortunately for Canada, USA were
able to break the tie with a fourth
goal. The last minute winner
scored by Alex Morgan broke
Canadian hearts, as it meant
that they wouldn't be making
it to the final. But all was not lost,
because in the Olympics, like many

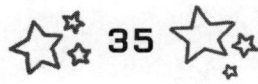

international football competitions, there is the third place play-off – a game between the two losing semi-finalist teams that decides who finishes third in the competition. And there was an additional cherry on top. Since this was the Olympics, the victor would also claim a bronze medal.

Having lost to Japan in the other semi-final, France would be Canada's opponents. They were a top European side with a host of talented players in their squad, so it would be a tough game. However, with this one last chance, the Canadian team wanted to make sure that they didn't return home empty-handed. France were a stubborn opponent, and neither side scored in ninety minutes. But in additional time, a goal was scored that was written into Canadian football folklore. Diana Matheson pounced on a loose ball and scored in the dying seconds of the game, giving Canada the lead with hardly any time left. Shortly after, the final whistle was blown and the game ended. The Canadian

 manager fell to his knees with joy, while the players on the pitch celebrated and cheered as loudly as they could. They might not have won the tournament, but they had taken Canada further in the competition than they had ever gone before. They had won the country its first bronze medal in the women's football event.

Jordyn watched with an uncontrollable smile as the players were awarded their medals. She already knew that she loved football,

but at that very moment, she chose to dedicate herself to it. Although she enjoyed ice hockey, this football tournament at the Olympics had awoken something deep inside her. Jordyn wanted to feel what the Canadian players were feeling. She wanted to play in those stadiums, fight for precious points and compete for her country on the world stage.

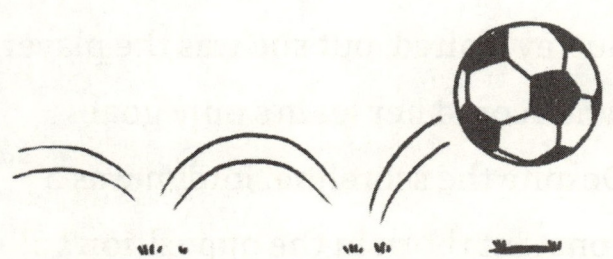

4

GETTING
SERIOUS

Jordyn joined her Chilliwack FC
teammates at a tournament being
held in Seattle. Her side lost 7-1 to
Surrey United, but she was the player
who scored her team's only goal.
Despite the scoreline, Jordyn was a
constant thorn in the opposition's

side. As a result, the
Surrey United team spoke
to Jordyn after the match
and asked if she would join them.
It was a difficult choice because
Jordyn loved playing at Chilliwack
FC, but she knew that this was an
opportunity that would push her
further. This could be the first of
many steps that would help her
achieve her new dream of making it
to the top.

Jordyn said her goodbyes to
Chilliwack FC and moved to Surrey
United. Although it was another local

team, it was further away from home and closer to the city of Vancouver. It was a team for developing players who wanted to push themselves by playing against others in competitive settings, taking the next step to see just how much talent a player possessed. Jordyn willingly made the move, but as she did, she made herself a promise: that even in a tougher setting, she would not allow herself to forget the reason why she played football. She did it because she loved it, and no one was going to take that enjoyment away.

Jordyn excelled in her new setting, quickly making new friends and developing her skills on the pitch at a staggering pace. It was from this point onwards that Jordyn's football career began to accelerate. Since she was playing for one of the top sides in the area, Jordyn came to the attention of scouts for the national team. When they called her in to attend a training camp with the Canadian national team, Jordyn couldn't believe it. She was over the moon! She had been inspired to play partly because of the national team's success, and now she would get her chance to play for one of her country's youth teams.

With an enormous smile on her face, Jordyn told her family and friends that she had been invited to play for the Canadian under 15s. And all while she was still only twelve years old! The scouts evidently saw something in her, believing that she was ready to play and train with players years older than her. And not only were they older, but they were also viewed as the best in the country for their age group.

Despite the age difference, Jordyn slotted right into life with the national team. The matches were harder and the training sessions were more intense, but Jordyn relished each and every challenge. She never shied away from any difficulty ahead of her and saw everything as a test or a way to develop her abilities. This fearless desire and exciting talent inspired everyone who watched her.

Before long, it was once again time for Jordyn to climb another rung on the ladder. She wanted to progress from Surrey United and join something even bigger – a club where she'd be able to test herself against the very best on a regular basis, just like the players she had played with at the national team camps. However, Jordyn's next step would come at a cost; it was a move that meant she would need to leave the comforts of home behind. For her next step, at the age of just fourteen, Jordyn set out on an adventure unlike anything she'd ever experienced before.

5
VANCOUVER WHITECAPS

In 2015, a new sporting programme was launched in Canada. A youth development network, run in partnership with the Vancouver Whitecaps, had been designed to help craft and mould the future of Canadian football. It was a safe

space for young girls and boys to improve their footballing abilities while maintaining a strong education. The idea was to develop the next generation of talent who would consistently finish tournaments with a place on the podium.

Players had to be invited to join the academy, and Jordyn was one of the first names on the list for the Girls Elite Rex programme. The course wasn't too far away from home, but it was a stretch for her to be able to commute every day. Instead, Jordyn left her home in Chilliwack to live in Burnaby, Vancouver. It was difficult to be away from home, but Jordyn loved her football and knew that this was a sacrifice she had to make. Plus, it certainly helped that she was a lively and playful character who got on well with people. This made it easy for her to settle into her new academy and instantly make friends. She was also a star student, often setting an extraordinary example for the rest of her peers.

As well as playing at the academy,

Jordyn was continually selected
to participate in Canadian youth
call-ups. As a reward for her talent,
dedication and outstanding abilities,
Jordyn was awarded with something
entirely out of the ordinary.
She was selected to train
alongside the Canadian
women's first team. When
the day finally came and Jordyn
arrived at the training ground, she
could hardly contain her excitement.
But as she caught sight of the first
team players, she suddenly felt a little
overwhelmed. Her excitement was

quickly replaced with fear and it felt
like her heart had stopped beating.
She needed to take a moment. Jordyn
hid in a little room to the side for
perhaps almost an hour, trying to
work up the courage to go and meet
them all. She had idolised so many of
these footballers for years and now
she was going to train with them –
an experience almost unheard of for
someone her age. It was a decision
made by the Canadian football
association to show just
how much they valued
her as a prospect, and

to show Jordyn just how high she could reach if she continued her rapid rise to footballing stardom. After some deep breaths, Jordyn finally composed herself and got stuck into the dream training session with the first team. She even got to meet Sinclair, who was her biggest idol and one of the best attacking women's players in the world. Sinclair introduced herself to Jordyn upon meeting her, but she certainly didn't need to. Jordyn knew exactly who she was, of course!

She still couldn't believe that she was in a training session alongside her idol.

Jordyn returned to training at the academy with a renewed energy and even greater determination to get back to that first team. If she wanted to become a Canadian national team starter, she would have to push her football harder and further. For most players Jordyn's age, it would normally take years to make it to  the top. But a player with her ability doesn't come around very often. And to

her surprise, and that of many others, it was not too long before she found herself playing for her country.

6
CANADIAN SENSATION

At the Vancouver Whitecaps, Jordyn dedicated herself to the constant pursuit of improvement. After each session, she aimed to find every little thing that she could improve on, and any advantage that she could use to help push herself in the right direction.

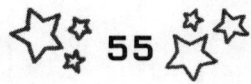

As a teenager, Jordyn was one of the academy's tallest players. Standing at 5 foot 11, she towered over most of her teammates. But unlike many tall players, Jordyn also possessed speed. With her height, her skill and her footballing brain, she appeared to have it all. It was great for a player to have talent, but it was exceptionally rare for a player to tick all of the boxes. This combination of attributes meant that Jordyn was

frequently involved with the Canadian national team setup. Before 2017,

Jordyn was thought of as a rising star in her local area, and her name was known only in a small circle of people. However, after the events of 2017, Jordyn's name would be one known across the country. Over the course of a year, she went from a secret talent to Canada's most promising prospect.

It all started with the U17s. At fifteen years old, Jordyn was selected to play for the Canadian U17s. During her stint with the team, she both impressed and scored. Later in the year, to give her more of a challenge,

Jordyn was invited to play with the U20s. To no one's surprise, she scored again and showed that she could cope with the higher standard of football. Yet it was during the next phase of her career that Jordyn broke records and ensured that her name was all over the Canadian media networks.

In the same year, Jordyn was invited to join the Canadian women's national first team. This time not as an additional player, or as a reward, or for experience. It was because she deserved it, and because the coach believed Jordyn was ready to play for the national team.

Jordyn made her national first team debut in the final of the Algarve Cup, an invitational tournament held every year in Portugal where some of the best countries in the world face off against one another. Jordyn played in the first half. And although she gave it everything she had, in the end Canada lost the final 1-0 to Spain. Despite the result, Jordyn had still done herself incredibly proud. She had become the third youngest player to debut for the Canadian women's national team.

It was in a friendly on the 11th of June 2017 that Jordyn really made a name for herself. It was also in this match that records were broken and discussions about her future would begin. In front of a large crowd at the BMO arena in Toronto, Canada, the Canadian team played a friendly match against Costa Rica.

 Jordyn started the match on the bench, but she watched in wonder as the team put

on an incredible performance.
The Canadians were 4-0 up in the
opening twenty-one minutes, easily
brushing their opponents aside and
putting on a spectacle for all
of the fans in attendance.
To Costa Rica's relief, no
more goals were scored for
a long period of the game. But as
the match reached the final twenty
minutes, Jordyn was called over by
the manager. She was asked to warm
up, because she was being brought
into the game. In a match already
filled with goals, there was a good

chance that Jordyn could score her first goal for the national first team today. She swiftly warmed up and was subbed onto the pitch in the 68th minute, replacing the iconic Sinclair as striker.

Only a few minutes later, Jessie Fleming, a talented Canadian midfielder, played a through ball into the opposition's box. Lawrence reached the ball and passed it across the goal line. Her accurate cross bypassed the goalkeeper entirely. Jordyn arrived at just the right time and jostled with a defender to get to the ball. It was hardly the most beautiful or technical of goals, but Jordyn was able to bundle the ball over the line with her thigh. She hardly knew what to do afterwards. It felt incredible to score her first goal for Canada, but it felt bittersweet because she had hardly done anything. All she had done was let the ball hit her and bounce over the line. It was Jordyn's first official goal for the national first team, but she wanted more. And it was with this feeling, this desire, that Jordyn created another opportunity for herself. Only one minute later, Jordyn sprinted into an attacking position. She reacted first to a deflected cross into the box and powerfully struck the ball at goal. Venting her frustrations over the first clumsy goal, she focussed them into an unstoppable strike. The ball flew into the back of the net with a satisfying thwack. This goal felt far greater than the first goal had. Now Jordyn truly felt like she had scored for the national team. She had helped her team to definitively finish the match with Canada emerging as the clear victors, with a commanding 6-0 win.

At the end of the match, Jordyn was invited to give a post-match interview to the media. She stood there in the full national team kit, smiling and talking to the presenter. But she was unaware of what her teammates were planning. They ran up behind her and poured water all over her head from their water bottles, soaking her

in front of the TV cameras! All Jordyn did was laugh; she truly felt like she was

a part of this Canadian national team. She had earned her spot in the squad for years to come. By scoring in this match, Jordyn became the first ever Canadian women's player to score for the U17s, U20s and first team in a calendar year. And her rapid rise to stardom had resulted in many fans calling her the next Christine Sinclair. This was something that Jordyn could hardly comprehend, having idolised

 the striker for years. She was still getting used to playing alongside Sinclair in training, let alone being

seen as her potential successor.
But outside all of the talk, hype and
excitement, there was a certainty
for Canada. They had an incredibly
talented young forward in their side.
With Jordyn, they had a promising
player who could make a huge impact
for this team in the years ahead.

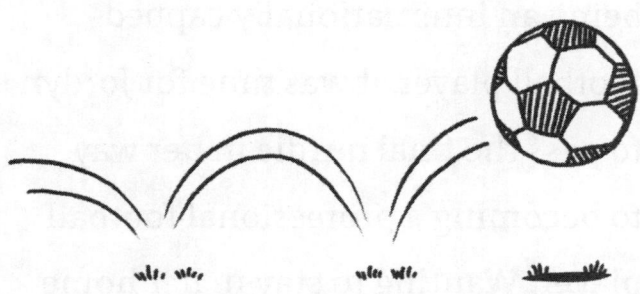

7

MAKING A DECISION

Having spent four years developing her game at the academy, and now being an internationally capped football player, it was time for Jordyn to pass the final hurdle in her way to becoming a professional football player. Wanting to stay in her home

country, Jordyn signed with the TSS
FC Rovers – a Canadian team that
played in Burnaby, which was where
Jordyn had settled and lived during
her academy years. But that wasn't the
only thing she wanted to do in the near
future. In Canada it was normal for
players to go and study at a university,
often over the border in the US where
there are highly competitive university
sports. Like all those before her, Jordyn
planned on doing the same. However,

 even the best plans and
ideas do not always play
out as expected. No one

could have predicted just how big a star Jordyn would become, or which exciting opportunities would land at her feet.

In 2018, Jordyn was playing for Canada against Japan in the fifth match of the Algarve Cup. In the crowd was a manager from one of the biggest European clubs and best sides in France, Paris Saint-Germain. They had not originally come to watch Jordyn or scout for potential players to sign. Instead, they had come to watch Ashley Lawrence – a

PSG player who was also playing for Canada. However, while Jordyn was on the pitch the PSG manager was completely distracted and did not pay much attention to Lawrence. With Jordyn, they could see an amazing talent performing right in front of them. And not only that, but they could also see that she was a gifted player who could be nurtured alongside the club's existing stars.

After the match, they got in touch with Jordyn and asked if she would consider coming to play for PSG.

The day had already been an incredible one for Jordyn. She had helped her country win the match and finish the tournament on a high, and now this! Until this moment, it looked like her future would be in Canada and university. But this offer could potentially change everything. Maybe her future wasn't in Canada, but in France. Jordyn thought carefully about the offer and confided in her parents, friends and coaches, trying not to rush into a hasty decision. After all, she still wanted to go to university. In the end,

 the thought of a life in Paris was too exciting to refuse. It was an incredible opportunity and one Jordyn wanted to take. But she didn't have to decide straight away, and she wouldn't necessarily have to miss out on university entirely. It was proposed that Jordyn should go and live in Paris for a few months, which meant that she would still have time to make a decision about going to university. She could see what living thousands of miles away in France was like first, before signing

on the dotted line and making a final decision. A decision that would change her career forever.

Jordyn had been lucky enough to travel and visit faraway places through football tournaments and family holidays. But this wasn't just a holiday, or a temporary stop in a hotel or villa, it was a move that needed serious consideration. Up to now, Jordyn had overcome any challenge put before her. If she put her mind to it, Jordyn believed that she could make this move a success. She decided to go for it.

Before long, the day of the move arrived. Jordyn said her goodbyes to her family and close friends, promising to come back and see them as soon as she could. With adventure on her mind, and her football boots packed in her suitcase, Jordyn boarded the aeroplane bound for Paris.

8
PARISIAN LIFE

Jordyn fell in love with the city of Paris. The language barrier was difficult, but living in a city known for its beauty helped her to get past it. She had swapped Canadian mountains and snow for the hustle and bustle of a capital city. She felt

like she was in the centre of everything and where she needed to be. While training with the team, during her 'taster' period with the club, it didn't take Jordyn too long to realise what her heart was set on. Although going to university was what everybody else did, Jordyn had an opportunity to achieve her dream right in front of her. She didn't want to study to become an architect, a doctor or a scientist. Jordyn wanted to be a footballer, and now she had the perfect opportunity. It was a once in a lifetime chance that many dream of but never get.

Women in football often feel like they have to have a backup profession. While the men's game is filled with money and big contracts, that is certainly not the case in the women's game. Many players often struggle to get by – even with professional deals. However, the tide has been changing in recent years. Although female players are still far from earning the enormous contracts male footballers receive,

 the money is increasing in the game to the point where many can consider football their only profession. It was with this shift in the women's game, and with a lot of courage, that Jordyn had made her decision. She was not going to university. She was going to be a professional footballer. That huge choice made her the first ever Canadian to turn pro coming straight out of high school.

At the start of 2019, Jordyn officially became a PSG player at just eighteen years old. She had the blessing of her family and friends, and her move to Paris was now permanent. She signed a four-year contract with a reasonable salary, which allowed her to settle into life far away from home. It was exciting for Jordyn to have an influx of money. She had always loved fashion and trainers, so she allowed herself a couple of treats. After that, Jordyn made sure that she was handling her incoming funds with care. She had to make sure that she spent it wisely and saved for her future. A footballer's career is short, often

spanning a range of only
ten to fifteen years, so it is
always important for players
to consider their future – no
matter how young or new to
the world of professional football
they are.

Jordyn joined PSG at the end of
the 2018/2019 campaign, giving her
plenty of time to train and settle
into her new life over the summer
of 2019. PSG were an ambitious side
competing in the top division of
French football, and they were always
on the hunt to capture the elusive

Division 1 title. The team often contested for their position at the top of the league, but they had never before finished as winners. By adding developing talents such as Jordyn to their ranks, the club were thinking of the future. They were trying to put a stop to their run of second, third and fourth place finishes by finding hungry and talented players who could help them reach the top.

However, before Jordyn could focus on club football, there was the small matter of a huge international tournament on the horizon. The Canadian squad for the 2019 World Cup had been announced. Jordyn, despite her youth and inexperience, had been selected as a member of the squad! She could hardly believe her luck when she heard the news. She had gotten into football to compete at the very top with the national team in major tournaments, and now she was going to her first one! She was going to be part of a team competing for the most sought-after trophy in football. France were

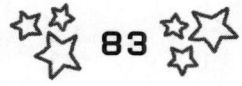

hosting the tournament, so Jordyn was already exactly where she needed to be. She was more than ready to do her best to help Canada achieve World Cup glory.

9
WORLD CUP 2019

Jordyn's national teammates joined her in France. They were all excited to reconnect, but also to come together for a bigger purpose: to try and get their country as far through the tournament as possible.

Jordyn wanted to savour every moment. It was her first major international competition, and because she was still so young there would hopefully be many more to come. She tried to soak in as much of the atmosphere and experience as she could, enjoying each training session, each fan interaction and every moment with her teammates. These were the days and matches that millions of players around the world dreamt of being involved with, and Jordyn didn't want to waste a single second of it.

Canada had been placed in Group E alongside Cameroon, New Zealand and the Netherlands. It was a challenging group, but certainly one that the team believed they could progress from. Cameroon were their first opponents, and the two sides played in a tight encounter. Canada's Kadeisha Buchanan scored the only goal of the match, helping them claim three points from their opening game of the group. As one of the youngest squad members, Jordyn did not play a part in the match, but

she also didn't *expect* to play much of a role in the tournament at all. Although Jordyn had earned her spot in the squad, she was still an inexperienced player compared with most of the others. There were many talented players who were older, more experienced and ahead of her in the team rankings. Jordyn was there as an option for the team and, as one of Canada's rising stars, it was also a chance for her to adapt to the World Cup experience. Learning from the ups and downs of a major international

 tournament would give her an advantage in the years ahead. The coaches certainly believed that Jordyn was going to be important to the future of Canadian football, and that she would be one of the country's leading lights.

Canada continued their strong start in the competition with a win in their second match. They defeated New Zealand 2-0 in an impressive showing. Goals from Fleming and Nichelle Prince put Canada in a strong position at the top of the group table.

Canada's third and final group stage match sadly did not go so well. Jordyn was given her World Cup debut in this match, but the team would be facing the toughest opponent in their group. The Netherlands were the winners of the UEFA Women's Euros in 2017, and they were one of the best teams in international football. Canada lost the match 2-1, but they still progressed into the knock-out rounds. It may not have been the perfect result, but it was a match that was beneficial in other ways.

For Jordyn, it had helped her to build her connections on the pitch. She had also gained crucial experience, which was an opportunity that many players her age could hardly expect to have.

The team's opponents for the round of 16, a knock-out round, were Sweden – an impressive European side that would pose a tough challenge to Jordyn and her teammates. Jordyn had to watch from the sidelines as her country were defeated 1-0 in the tie. A goal from Stina Blackstenius was enough to help Sweden through to the quarter-finals and eliminate Canada from the competition.

Jordyn was extremely disappointed that the tournament was over for Canada. It felt like she had so much more to give and that the team had the ability and strength to go further.

But in football, things do not always go as everyone hopes. In the end, there can only be one winner. Jordyn had learnt a lot from this experience, and she couldn't wait to get back on the pitch for her country.

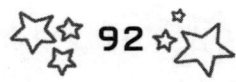

At the next tournament, she wanted more game time. She didn't want to be on the bench, watching the game unfold, unable to affect it. Next time, she was going to be on that pitch, helping her country go further than ever before. She wanted to finish as a winner, with a medal around her neck and a trophy lifted in the air, watching red and white confetti fall from the stadium's rooftop.

10
DIVISION 1 CHAMPIONS

With her World Cup experience behind her, Jordyn returned to Paris to prepare for her first season with PSG. While game time had been hard to come by for her country, the same could not be said at PSG. Jordyn was thrown straight into the deep end with matches for her club, playing in the majority of the team's games in the league and cup competitions.

Jordyn also had her best ever spell with the national team during this period. She played a crucial role in helping her country qualify for the Olympics. Canada competed in the CONCACAF Olympic Qualifying Championship, a short tournament held between the best ranked nations from North America, Central America and the Caribbean to decide who goes to the Olympics.

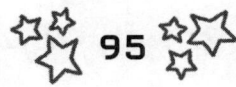

Encouraged by the inspirational memories of London 2012, Jordyn played a crucial role in the team's qualification. She scored seven goals, a leading tally for the competition, and helped Canada to qualify for Tokyo 2020.

She returned to PSG to finish the season. The team had been playing well and Jordyn was a big part of it, making nineteen appearances and scoring five goals. She hoped to push PSG towards their first league title, followed by a summer that she'd always

 dreamt of: representing Canada at the Olympics.

But this was not to be.

In March 2020, the COVID-19 pandemic brought football in France to a halt. In fact, almost everything in the world was brought to a halt, and many countries went into an enforced lockdown. So, to avoid being trapped in France, Jordyn returned to Canada to be with her family during this scary time. At first, no one knew just how long the pandemic would last. Jordyn expected to stay at home for only a couple of weeks, but that quickly became longer. Weeks turned into months, and Jordyn's life was turned completely upside down. The Olympics were postponed, and Jordyn had to exercise in her back garden instead of spending her time playing football. She took part in numerous video calls with PSG's physios and coaches to maintain her fitness. Although this was a challenging time, being at home had some benefits too. For the first time in years, Jordyn was able to spend quality time with her family, reconnecting and sharing stories about her time away.

After a handful of months, Jordyn was able to return to France. But things did not return to normality – far from it. Instead, the world had completely changed. Jordyn was able to train with her teammates, but she had to be tested at the start of every single session to ensure that she didn't have the COVID-19 coronavirus.

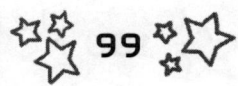

The 2020/2021 Division 1 season was unlike any other, because

99

fans were not allowed into stadiums to watch football. Instead, matches had to take place in empty stadiums with fans watching through their TV screens or listening on radios. Despite this, something special was happening at PSG. After some time away, the squad had come back more determined than ever and with a stronger sense of team spirit. With this newfound bond, PSG just couldn't stop winning. Defeating

opponent after opponent, their incredible run just did not stop. With Jordyn's help, for the first time in the club's history, PSG were crowned champions of Division 1.

But at the end of the regular season, Jordyn's work was still not over. In the summer of 2021, Jordyn was named in Canada's squad for the postponed Olympics. She was a year older, wiser and more experienced, ready to use everything she had learnt to help her country. Jordyn dreamt of not only matching the bronze medal of London 2012, but of going even further, to dream even

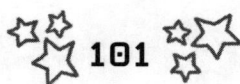

bigger. Perhaps, if everyone came together, Canada could go for gold ...

11
TOKYO 2020

The Tokyo 2020 Olympics were
unlike any other in the history of
the games. Due to the aftermath
of COVID-19, it was the first one
ever to have little or no crowds in
attendance. Instead, fans watched
on TVs as the greatest athletes in the
world competed against one another

in empty stadiums. But that was no problem for Jordyn. She had shown that she could play at her best even in the strangest of circumstances. All she needed was her team by her side and the knowledge that her family were watching from afar.

Canada had entered this tournament as underdogs. There were so many talented countries in the competition: the USA, Brazil, Norway and not to forget the hosts, Japan, who were backed by an entire nation and playing in familiar surroundings.

Yet the title of underdogs didn't matter to the Canadian team. There was an incredible feeling and buzz within the squad, with many dreaming and believing that Canada would make an impact at this tournament. The country had never gone further than achieving a bronze medal. Perhaps this was the year that the country could change that.

Canada had been placed in Group E with Japan, Chile and Great Britain. This was a tough group and gaining points was going to be tricky, but

Jordyn and her teammates believed that they had a good chance. The team started the tournament with a hard match against Japan. A goal from Sinclair helped Canada to a 1-1 draw and a strong opening performance. Many had thought that Japan would win, but the Canadian team showed the world exactly what they were made of. They were here to be serious contenders, and no one was going to push them around.

The second match of the group was against Chile. Canada were able

to overcome their South American opponents with a 1-2 victory, which was swiftly followed by a 1-1 draw against Great Britain. This result confirmed Canada's place in the knock-out rounds of the competition, which is the point in tournaments where teams face either victory or elimination.

Canada had been drawn against Brazil at the quarter-final stage. Brazil were a team filled with talented  tricksters and legends of the women's game, so Canada would need to play to the best of their ability to progress further. Neither side could score in the first ninety minutes, and extra time had to be played. But again, neither could score. The match had to be settled by penalties. Jordyn was on the pitch at the time, but she was not one of the first five penalty takers. All she could do was watch as her teammates walked up to the spot. After a tense shootout, Canada won 4-3 on penalties and emerged victorious. The Canadian goalkeeper, Stephanie Labbé, was the hero of the

match, saving two of Brazil's penalties to help Canada make it to the semi-final of the Olympics.

It was a familiar foe that Jordyn and Canada had to face in the semi-finals. They had been drawn against the favourites for the competition and their southern neighbours, the USA. Canada went into the match as underdogs, but they had every belief that they could cause an upset. The USA were dominant for the majority of the match but they were unable to score. Canada's resolute defence kept their opponents at bay and gave their side a chance. That chance came in the form of a penalty in the 75th minute. Fleming fired the ball into the back of the net and ran off to celebrate with her teammates. To the surprise of many, Canada were able to hold onto the lead and knock the USA out of the competition, beating their rivals for the first time in twenty years! This team were breaking new ground for Canadian football. Never

before had this side gone further than a third place finish. They had booked their place in the final and had a very real chance of winning it. The only thing standing in their way was a Swedish side who also had their hearts set on a gold medal.

The match kicked off at the Nissan Stadium in Yokohama, with both teams desperate to make history for their country. The start of the match was a cagey affair, but this was to be expected; it was a game between two of the best defences in the tournament. But in the 34th minute, one of those defences was breached. Sweden's Blackstenius poked the ball past Labbé to give Sweden a 1-0 lead. On the bench, Jordyn could do nothing but watch. She desperately hoped that her team could get back into the final, and she made sure that she was ready to come on if she was needed.

Canada searched for a way back into the game and found it in the 66th minute when Sinclair was fouled in the box. Canada were awarded a

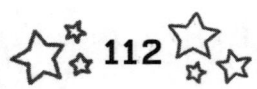 penalty. As she had done all tournament, Fleming coolly slotted the ball into the net and levelled

the score at 1-1. Jordyn was substituted onto the pitch late in the game. She swapped places with the tired Sinclair, who had given her all for the team. Jordyn tried her best, constantly threatening the Swedish defence, but neither side could find a winner in regular or extra time. The final was going to be settled by penalties.

The pressure of the situation got to the two teams, and they both only scored two out of five of their penalties. This meant that the penalties were going to sudden

death, which is when both teams get one chance each to win the match by taking it in turns to try and score a penalty. The first team to score when the other team miss are the winners. Sweden's Jonna Andersson stepped up to take the penalty, but she missed. Now it was Canada's turn, and it was Julia Grosso with the opportunity. Grosso was one of Jordyn's closest friends, and the pair had grown up together through the Canadian youth teams. Jordyn stood at the halfway line, wishing with all her heart that her friend could win it all. Grosso took a moment to compose herself, before running up to the ball and striking it at goal. The Swedish goalkeeper guessed the right way, and Jordyn could hardly watch as the ball hit the goalkeeper's glove. But it wasn't over. The strike was so strong that it had enough power to push past the goalkeeper's hand, rebounding up into the air and smashing against the roof of the net. Canada had done it! Jordyn and the rest of the team ran over to Grosso. The gold medal was theirs. They were Olympic champions!

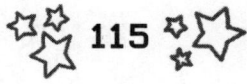

12
OL REIGN

Jordyn returned to Paris with her newly acquired gold medal, ready for the 2021/2022 season. By this point, she had helped PSG win the Division 1 title and made a dream come true with Canada at the Olympics. It felt like her career was taking off. Jordyn was meeting the expectations

that had been set for her, realising her early promise. She believed that her career at PSG would continue to build on her success, but that wasn't quite the case. PSG had a squad filled with talented players, and the club had been able to recruit even more talent during the summer transfer window because of their success. Jordyn found game time hard to come by in the 2021/2022 season. She had spent many years developing at the club, and it was also where she had experienced her breakthrough.

While she was still young, just twenty years old, Jordyn felt that she needed to play more frequently. In order to improve her football, she had to have more opportunities on the pitch. But it became clear that those opportunities were not coming Jordyn's way at PSG, so she decided that it was time for a change. She wanted to join a new club where she could get more game time.

At the end of the season, there were many teams on the hunt for someone of her talents. Jordyn was signed by

OL Reign, a team that competes in the National Women's Soccer League (known as the NWSL) in the USA. Jordyn said her goodbyes to her Paris teammates, and then she left to embark on an exciting new adventure in the USA. It was difficult to say goodbye to a place where she had so many fond memories, and to all her teammates and friends at the club. But Jordyn knew that she was making the right decision. It was time for something new.

Jordyn settled into life in Seattle. She was welcomed by all of her new teammates and fitted in with ease. She was able to play with talented players such as Megan Rapinoe, Rose Lavelle and Quinn. Jordyn also achieved her wish of getting more game time. During the 2022 season, Jordyn played in over half of the team's league matches. She also scored twice during her debut season at the club, helping the team to finish in first place during the regular season and claim the NWSL Shield.

Jordyn had made a brave decision to leave PSG, as they were a quality side competing at the top of French football, but she had made a decision that was right for her. Joining OL Reign, a talented side in the USA, meant that she could bring joy and happiness back to her game – the reason she played football in the first place.

13
CANADA'S FUTURE

Jordyn is now playing football with a constant smile, loving each and every training session, match and competition. She is a key player for OL Reign and hopes that she can help the club win more NWSL Shields. She also hopes to go one step further and win the NWSL Championships in the play-offs.

She has come so far from the teenager who left Canada to live in France. Jordyn has developed so many aspects of her game and is starting to live up to her full potential. With Canada's record goalscorer, Sinclair, coming to the end of her career, it will be up to Jordyn to become the next striking sensation who helps her country achieve the unimaginable on the world stage. Of course, two players are never entirely

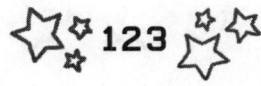

comparable, and it is unfair to label Jordyn as the next Sinclair. Quite simply, she is Jordyn Huitema – nothing more, nothing less. She has her own skills and her own talents, which will no doubt be on display in future fixtures.

Jordyn will surely play a large part in the upcoming World Cup in Australia and New Zealand, where Canada will try their best to succeed in the tournament. The best footballers from around the world will play for their countries and compete for the right to be called champions. Usually an underdog, but with an Olympic victory in their pocket, Canada will head to the tournament with high hopes. There are many top-level national football teams, and Canada can certainly class themselves among them. Jordyn and the rest of her teammates will do their best to help Canada get as far in the tournament as possible.

No matter how Canada perform, one thing is for certain. They have one of the most promising rising stars in world football in their team.

 Jordyn is a footballer who plays the game not for the money or the fame, but because of her pure love and enthusiasm for the sport. She still plays football as if she's messing around in the back garden with her brothers, or running riot on the pitch at Chilliwack FC, or impressing the crowds at her matches for Surrey United.

Many coaches have spoken about her future, and about all of the great things that she will go on to achieve. She is a once in a generation talent

who possesses all of the qualities needed for success. Jordyn has proven time and time again that she is capable of living up to those expectations, but she has also shown that she won't let anyone else decide her future for her. Her future will not be decided by newspaper speculation, rumours or pressure. Her future is now firmly under her own control. Jordyn will decide where *she* wants to play, who *she* wants to play with, and what environment *she* needs to perform at her best. All she wants is to continue playing football with

the same childish joy that she felt all of those years ago, never losing sight of the young girl who fell in love with the game on the football pitches of British Columbia.